Herbal Apothecary

The Best Herbal Medicine and How to Grow and Use to Self Healing

The information in the following pages is broadly considered to be a truthful and accurate account of facts and as such any inattention, use or misuse of the information in question by the reader will render any resulting actions solely under their purview. There are no scenarios in which the publisher or the original author of this work can be in any fashion deemed liable for any hardship or damages that may befall them after undertaking information described herein.

Additionally, the information in the following pages is intended only for informational purposes and should thus be thought of as universal. As befitting its nature, it is presented without assurance regarding its prolonged validity or interim quality. Trademarks that are mentioned are done without written consent and can in no way be considered an endorsement from the trademark holder.

Table of Contents

Introduction

Congratulations on downloading *Herbal Apothecary* and thank you for doing so.

The following chapters will discuss herbs that you can grow in your garden that have some medicinal benefits and those that can possibly help alleviate some issues that are relatively common, and maybe some other issues that are not so common. In addition to providing information about the herbs, information on proper drying, gardening, and storage of herbs are also included. The use of herbs in treating ailments dates back thousands of years and has been a tradition for several cultures around the world, but information on their use how to grow them and how to ensure home-grown quality can be difficult to find. With the vast number of supplements available in your local vitamin store and online, it can be overwhelming for someone new to alternative healthcare. Sometimes, you just don't know where to start.

There are plenty of books on this subject on the market, thanks again for choosing this one! Every effort was made to ensure it is full of as much useful information as possible, please enjoy!

Chapter 1: The History of Herbal Medicine

From several various sources, we can trace man's use of plants and herbs for medicine as far back as mankind itself. In fact, a number of drugs on the market today are based in folk medicine from the herbal world. Herbal medicines are made from whole plants or parts of a plant. Also known as botanical medicines, supplements or sometimes remedies. Although these types of treatments are becoming more integrated into main-stream medical treatments, typically herbal medicine has been a self-treatment route for minor symptoms and non-life-threatening diseases. However, a lot of the drugs available on the market for treatment and alleviation of pain, are based on herbal or botanical materials. Examples of these are: aspirin, digitalis, atropine, morphine, quinine, and more. Research is happening every day to take what nature has done and extract the benefits

Some of the oldest written evidence of herbal medicine can be dated back to Sumeria about 5000 years ago. The Chinese had a book of 365 herbal medicine that was used around 2500 BC. The Ebers Papyrus, written around 1550 BC, is a collection of applications of herbal medicine representing about 700 plant species including Aloe Vera, castor oil, pomegranate, willow, fig, garlic, juniper, and more. Before the sixteenth century, a common practice in healing was to use the body's ability to heal itself and to supplement that with the right herbs. Monasteries traditionally had entire gardens devoted to growing the type of herbs that could be used to treat the public because healing was included in the responsibilities of the religious people. The monks were generally more educated than the general public, so they gathered information on the correct cultivating and harvesting practices, beneficial properties of the herb, as well as having access to importing plants not native to the area. This allowed them to expand their repertoire of treatments available.

One of the quintessential sources on herbal medicine, Culpeper's *The Complete Herbal*, was published in 1649 and has gone through over 100 editions. Since Culpeper was British, he focused on British plants and published his guide in English so that the reference guide could be of use to the public (at the time most reference guides were published in Latin, but Culpeper felt this would greatly reduce the audience of the guide). Although his guide was incredibly useful, it angered the medical establishments because herbal apothecaries were sometimes the more affordable healthcare for the general public, thus the doctors thought it was stealing their business. Unfortunately, Culpeper died at the age of 38 from tuberculosis.

As society progressed out of the Middle Ages, new plants from the Americas became known and their benefits were discovered and integrated into use as well. Over the next century, gardening radically changed as a number of new plants and seeds were discovered and brought back to be cultivated into main-stream usage. One of the first botanical gardens used for studying the plants was established at Oxford in 1621. It allowed the study of the use of herbs as medicinal treatments. This paved the way for herbs to enter the mainstream market and accelerated the spread of their health benefits to doctors and to the public.

In recent years, herbal healing has seen a new rise in popularity given the new age culture and interest in "alternative" or "holistic" medicine. Herbal treatments allow the public to essentially participate in their own self-care and keep treatments on a more natural basis. Although there are more references now about herbal medicines than 60 years ago, it is still worth the time of consumers to do a little homework before investing in supplements or other holistic treatments. Supplements are not regulated in the same way as traditional pharmaceutical medicines, so there might be a lot of products on the market that are not of the best quality and are not the most effective treatment for your ailment. With supplements, the quality and quantity can make a big difference as can the application; taking a supplement versus consuming an herbal tea can have a different effect– so it pays to be informed. And this may drive some followers of alternative medicine to pursue growing and dispensing the herbs themselves. In order for this to be the best experience, the consumer needs to understand each herb or plant, how it is best used (tincture, tea, supplement, poultice, etc.), the growing conditions, time of harvest, the manner of extraction, the manner of preparation and other details.

Note: All herbs should be used with caution because they contain powerful bioactive compounds. Start with small quantities initially to test your tolerance. Watch out for allergic reactions. People who have ragweed allergy may have similar reactions to medicinal plants belonging to that family.

When you feel good with a recommended amount of a given herb, it doesn't necessarily mean that you will feel better with larger quantities or a stronger brew. To derive maximum benefit out of the herbs you grow, try to learn as much about them as you can.

Chapter 2: Easy Herbs to Grow in Your Garden

There are a number of people with green thumbs who are capable of growing anything. But for those that struggle to make a flower bloom, there is still hope that you can grow, will flourish, and can then be used at home to the best benefits.

1. **Alfalfa** (*Medicago sativa*):

Although alfalfa is an herb, most people are familiar with it as a primary food source for farm animals. Which actually makes sense because alfalfa is recognized as one of the most nutritious food forages available. For humans, that holds true in addition to a number of actual health benefits. One of the reasons alfalfas rank is so high on the list of beneficial herbs is because the body can easily absorb and put the nutrients found in this plant to use. Alfalfa can help with a lot of issues like nausea, urinary tract problems (prostate, infections, or kidney stones), cleansing of toxins found in the liver, cholesterol, allergies, tooth decay, milk supply for nursing, cleans the blood,

blood clotting, pituitary gland, blood sugar levels, and more. Combined with sage, it may even ease menopause symptoms as it boosts the pituitary. It is a good daily source of minerals like iron, potassium, calcium, sulfur, phosphorous, and magnesium and vitamins A, C, E and K4. In addition, there are a number of essential amino acids that the body doesn't produce on its own, so we must get them from food. Alfalfa is a good source of these essential amino acids. If you are a fan of the green powders available for morning smoothies, alfalfa is frequently used as a base ingredient of those because it is so easy to use and digest, and it contains high chlorophyll contents.

Alfalfa is a perennial crop that is a good cover crop or soil conditioner. If you have a spot in your garden that seems soil depleted, plant alfalfa in that corner for a year or two. It is a drought resistant plant. In fact, it doesn't like being too wet for that can lead to mold growth. Choose an area with a lot of all-day sun and proper drainage. They do not require deep planting and the form roots rather quickly. Sow the seeds about one-half inch (.5") deep and cover lightly. Sprouts will appear in about 7-10 days. Thin the seeds as needed to give them a little growing room. Harvest for use before the purple blooms appear.

If you plan to grow alfalfa indoors, you can easily use a small jar or pot base and produce a much smaller crop. One tablespoon of seeds will produce about 1.5 cups of alfalfa. Wash the seeds you plan to use and remove any broken or discolored seeds. Place the washed seeds into a glass quart jar. Cover the prepared seeds with about two (2) inches of cold water; make sure they are completely covered. Do not use a metal lid but cover the jar with a small piece of cheesecloth; you can secure with a rubber band to keep the cloth tight. Keep the jar in a warm place for about 12 hours. Filtered sunlight is helpful, but direct sunlight is not necessary. Drain the water, rinse, and drain again. Tilt the jar on its side and place in a dark location that is warm. Spread the seeds out. Rinse the seeds again every 8-12 hours, draining well after each rinse. Do this for about four (4) days or until the seeds sprout and are about two (2) inches long. Spread the sprouts out into a thin layer on a flat surface and put them in a sunny location, wait for about 15 minutes for the leaves to turn green and the enzymes to activate. Now they're ready to be used on salads, sandwiches, or just to snack on.

A great alternative is to use the base of a clay pot; spread the soaked seeds on this base and put the base into a larger, shallow container of water. The clay will absorb enough water to keep the seeds hydrated. Make sure you use quality water and it will keep the plants as nutritional as possible. If you want to remove the coats from the sprouts, you just need to put them in a bowl of water and agitate the water briefly. The seed coats float to the top and you can take them out, leaving the hulled sprouts behind. You can use the sprouts fresh or keep them in the refrigerator.

Alfalfa is typically grown for feed or for use in the kitchen, it is not typically used as a decorative, flowering plant.

2. <u>Aloe Vera</u> (*A. barbadensis* Mill.):

This plant has a history of being a go-to source for treating burns and skin irritation when applied topically. However, aloe can also act as a helpful laxative when consumed and, in fact, has a myriad of healing properties. It has antibacterial, antifungal, and antiviral properties. It also can be used to relax the bowels and alleviate stomachaches.

For home use, it is generally safe and requires no processing before use. Aloe can be grown in almost any garden, either in pots or in the ground. They do well in a sunny location and in warm areas where frost wouldn't be an issue. It is a member of the succulent family, so it is drought resistant and it requires little watering, little care, and can thrive even in poor soil. Although there are several varieties of aloe, make sure you get Aloe Vera to ensure you get a plant with medicinal properties that would be edible.

When you have a burn, aloe can be a quick treatment. Snap off a piece and use the jelly-like, colorless pulp to smear onto the burn. This acts as an anti-inflammatory and antimicrobial ointment.   It is incredibly easy to use it for consumption as well. Wash the Aloe Vera leaf, cut it open, and scoop out the gel (gel should be clear; discard any greenish gel). Store the aloe in a glass jar and refrigerate for use. Add 2 teaspoons of gel to filtered water or any type of fruit juice. Regular ingestion can help prevent or relieve constipation and other digestive problems, which can include ulcerative colitis and irritable bowel syndrome.

Aloe Vera plants can be really carefree house plants. They can be grown indoors in pots even without a green thumb. The soil should be allowed to dry in between watering to discourage rot. Water the plant approximately every 21 days but even more sparingly during the winter. This plant does not require a lot of fertilizer. You may put fertilizer for no more than once a month only in spring and summer. It will probably need repotting when it becomes root bound and use a potting soil specifically developed for succulents.

Aloe Vera can be an attractive succulent grown in houseplants on the kitchen windowsill. With its long, slender, star-like appearance, it can add some pretty greenery to any corner.

3. <u>Cayenne</u> (*Capsicum annuum*):

This is a hemostatic herb that can help to stop bleeding. It might be an organic substitute for a baby aspirin to slow the progression of a heart attack. In addition, cayenne may serve to boost metabolism as it raises the amount of heat your body produces so that you naturally burn more calories in a day. A small boost, but when dieting and watching calories, every little bit of assistance can help. Some studies show that the capsaicin may also help to reduce hunger, which further helps to reduce the amount of caloric intake every day.

This well-known addition to your diet may even help to reduce high blood pressure, although current research has only been conducted with animals. Cayenne may also benefit your stomach in a way that isn't just good tasting, as it may actually boost the enzymes in your stomach which aid in digestion. Contrary to popular belief which warns against consuming spicy foods, cayenne may actually serve as a protection against ulcers. Capsaicin is also a common ingredient in most muscle rubs and creams that help to reduce aches and soreness. The symptoms of Psoriasis, an autoimmune disease that manifests in patches of scaly and red skin, can sometimes be alleviated by capsaicin.

A lot of people grow a variety of peppers in their garden and for good reason. They are easy to grow and easy to use. Chilies are sub-tropical and mostly perennial and they like heat. If you live in a climate that is consistently warm enough, plant them outside. Otherwise, you can put them in a pot and bring them indoors when necessary. Seeds should be planted in a sunny location in soil that drains well. If planting outside, seeds should be initially planted inside and transferred outdoors. Generally, transplanting should occur about seven (7) weeks after the seeds are sown. Moist soil is required, but take care not to add too much water.

Peppers are typically added to a garden for the produce; not for appearance. However, the plants themselves can be quite beautiful with their shocking red peppers. In fact, a number of ornamental peppers plants have been marketed just because of the appearance. This can add a bright splash of color to any kitchen.

4. <u>Chamomile</u> (*Chamaemelum nobile*):

With a lovely scent, this herb is most well known as a tea for relaxation. Most people drink it at the end of the day to calm down, ease stress, and some women use it to relieve menstrual cramps. In addition, it can be used to soothe a baby crying from colic. A tincture from flowers can also be used as a gargle to help with canker or mouth ulcers. People who suffer from eczema can use the cooled tea as a compress to ease symptoms. An anti-inflammatory, chamomile is less commonly used to treat digestive issues, improve the function of the liver, cleanse the blood, treat skin blisters, alleviate arthritis pain, and boost the pancreas. Drinking chamomile tea at night will promote a more restful sleep. The most effective and useful type is the Roman chamomile. The daisy type of flowers is a pretty addition to pots or a garden as well.

In the garden, sow the seeds in the Spring or Fall as chamomile prefers cool soil. It needs light, so scatter the seeds, but do not bury in the soil. Place them in an area that is full sun. Mature plants should be ready for use in about 90 days. Although you can get a jumpstart if you establish plants from another plant rather than from seeds. Once established, it takes very little care, as do most herbs. The herb is drought tolerant. It's a good plant to put around the outside of a garden as the potent scent can sometimes keep pests away.

Chamomile is a beautiful, flowering plant and if you are fond of daisies, you will be fond of seeing this sprouting in your backyard as well. With the cluster of small white flowers and relaxing smell, this is a definite bonus for any edging, garden, or flower bed.

5. <u>Dandelion</u> (*Taraxacum*):

Another weed that is super simple to grow and most people do so without ever intending to. It's good for treating liver and kidney issues as it's a diuretic in addition to supporting digestion and promoting hormone health. As the plant is edible, it's easy to add the greens to salads or to make a tea from the flowers. Dandelion is a good source of a variety of nutrients, and the leaves and roots contain vitamins like A, C, K and B-vitamins as well as minerals including magnesium, zinc, potassium, iron, calcium, and choline. Other parts of the plant can be used in various herbal remedies and almost every lawn has these flowers popping up. While you can put the leaves into a salad, you can brew the flowers into tea or even into wine (although that has fewer health benefits). Since the dandelion is high in zinc and magnesium, it can be used to treat skin conditions.

Almost everyone from a child to grandpa can recognize a dandelion flower. Those bright yellow heads that poke up in early spring. Most people who take care of a yard can rolls their eyes and sigh when seeing a sea of yellow starting to spread across the yard. But those plants should be a welcome sight to anyone using herbal medicine and natural teas.

6. <u>Echinacea</u> (*Echinacea purpurea*):

Echinacea is a steadfast staple in native North American herbal medicine. It helps the body fight both bacterial and viral infections. The fields across America host an array of flowers, some just pretty and some pretty useful. Echinacea, or the purple coneflower (*Echinacea purpurea*), is one of the best. Historically, Native Americans used the roots to treat a variety of issues from an insect bite to a snake bite. More recently, the flower buds have made their way into alternative treatments for a cold or the flu. A tincture made with alcohol is considered more potent; steep the flower buds or roots, or both, in pure, concentrated alcohol for 4-6 weeks, and then filter out the liquid. Echinacea is believed to be a natural defense mechanism that boosts the white blood cells, assisting your body in combating infections and bacteria.

Most commonly, Echinacea is grown best outside in a garden. Plants bloom heavily from July through September and can make your garden a haven for both butterflies and bees. Standing tall at 3-4 feet, they make a bright, eye-catching border. To thrive, plants should be planted in full sun, in a rich soil with good drainage because they only require a small amount of water but they will endure most conditions. These biennial plants flower only in the second season. To extend the blooming season, pinch off finished flowers on a regular basis.

With the pastel flowers of Echinacea, it is a welcome addition to your backyard. The daisy shaped flowers have a high, spiky seed cone and last about a month when they bloom. This can add a nice splash of color and pleasing aroma to any flower bed.

7. **<u>Garlic</u>** (*Allium sativum*):

Garlic is a well-known herb when it comes to both heart health and cooking. A member of the onion family, it is closely related to leeks, shallots, and onions. As is it so prevalent in cooking, the use of garlic for medicinal and health benefits goes back into ancient history. Perhaps the most beneficial elements of garlic are the sulfur compounds that are released, however, this means that ingestion must occur shortly after it is crushed. Garlic is an anti-bacterial, anti-parasitic, and anti-septic that can help purify the blood and promote healthy circulation. It may also help to balance blood sugar levels. In addition to the medicinal benefits, garlic contains a number of vitamins and minerals (B6, C, manganese, selenium) but very few calories. Regular usage of garlic as a supplement has been shown to boost your immune system and lower high blood pressure and cholesterol levels. In addition, studies suggest that it is a powerful antioxidant. Historically, garlic has been used by athletes in the Olympic games of ancient Greece to reduce fatigue and boost energy. The sulfur compounds in garlic may also help to protect against organ damage from heavy metal toxicity. Garlic has also been used as an ingredient in remedies for yeast infections, heart problems, asthma and sinus infections, and to fight bone loss.

Growing your own garlic may be one of the easiest home gardening projects. Softneck bulbs are typically found in most grocery stores and are the easiest to grow in mild regions. If you are planting inside, this is the type of bulb you would probably choose. If you are planting outdoors, you can choose softneck if you are in a mild climate. But may want to choose hardnecks if you have a real winter as they may not produce sufficient bulbs in warm climates. You may also want to choose the hardneck variety because you can also use their flower buds (scapes) as greens. For outdoors, planting usually occurs in mid-fall. Cloves should be inserted root-side down, spacing them at around eight (8) inches apart, and burying them about two (2) inches down. The bulbs are ready for harvesting when the lower leaves have browned but the upper leaves still look green. Gently remove the bulbs from the soil. If you are planting indoors or in a container, make sure that the bulb has plenty of room to spread out. The container should be placed in a spot that gets at least 6 hours of direct sunlight per day. Make sure the container drains well. Again, they should be harvested gently, and the bulbs can then be used in a variety of cooking or eaten raw for health benefits. However, as a daily supplement, it is best to obtain quality capsules from your local reputable health food or vitamin shop.

8. <u>Ginger</u> (*Zingiber officinale*):

Ginger is a popular treatment for an upset stomach; it slows the production of serotonin, a chemical trigger for nausea. It can stop vomiting and alleviate general nausea and motion sickness. It is also used to treat indigestion and circulatory problems. Chewing raw ginger or drinking a tea made from ginger or containing ginger can help. Ginger is a natural ingredient that can be an effective weapon in the fight against morning sickness since it is safe to use even during pregnancy. Ginger tea can also help when suffering from a cold or the flu. Ginger promotes sweating and warms the body from within allowing it to alleviate fever or chills. In addition, ginger may be helpful in reducing inflammation, pain associated with a menstrual cycle, cholesterol, risk of blood clotting, and high sugar levels in the blood.

To make ginger tea at home, simply slice about 30 grams of fresh ginger and steep it in hot water for a few minutes. You can add a slice of lemon to boost vitamin C levels as well or add honey for a little sweetness.

As long as you remember that ginger is a tropical plant and it likes hot and humid areas, it is easy to grow your own ginger in your kitchen. Start with a living ginger root. Select a root with tight skin that is firm and plump. Root should have several eye buds as well. Soak the ginger root in warm water overnight to prepare for planting. Since the roots will grow horizontally, choose a wide, shallow pot and fill it with well-draining potting soil. Insert the ginger root with the eye bud pointing up and cover it with 1-2 inches more of soil. Water the root lightly. Make sure the pot stays warm and doesn't get a lot of bright light, keep the soil moist, but not soaking wet. This is a slow process, so it may take 2-3 weeks before you see shoots coming up.

9. **<u>Great Mullein</u>** (*Verbascum thapsus*):

The medicinal benefits of mullein can date back to the early American settlers who brought it over from Europe because of it capability help treat various ailments like diarrhea and coughs. The utilization of the plant as medicinal treatment spread from the settlers to the Native Americans. Both the flowers and leaves can be used in various treatments, primarily related to respiratory tract problems. Tea made from the leaves and flowers can be used as an expectorant to relieve coughs associated with ailments such as bronchitis. Believe it or not, smoking the mullein leaves has been used to relieve chest congestion as the plant helps to loosen phlegm and flush out the lungs.

Some of the potential benefits of mullein are for the following: warts, athlete's foot, cough, skin infections, sore throat, asthma, bronchitis, and more. You can crush the mullein flowers to make a paste, put it on a wound and it will work as an antiseptic. It also has antiviral properties that may help to ease symptoms associated with a viral infection. Drinking mullein tea may also help to reduce bad cholesterol levels which reduces the risk of high blood pressure and other heart diseases. Extract from the flower can be added to hair rinses to help keep the scalp healthy, stop dandruff, and will naturally enhance your hair's color.

Even if you have very little gardening experience, mullein is a great plant to start with because it is easy to grow and maintain. Since it is classified as a weed, the plant thrives almost anywhere. Place seeds about 18 inches apart in a garden bed on top of the soil. The area should have good drainage because mullein doesn't like excessively moist soil. If possible, plant in an area with access to direct sunlight. The plants need very little watering; never keep the soil soggy. Definitely, give them room as the stalks can grow for as long as seven (7) feet tall.

Make sure you remove the rosettes as they grow, or you will have all the seeds (100,000+) sowing on the wind where they can lay dormant for many years. If multiple rosettes form and all those seeds spread and then grow, you might end up with a big mullein population on your hands.

With pretty yellow flowers and fuzzy leaves, this plant can make a great border, but make sure you plant them in the back as they can grow taller than some people.

10. <u>Lavender</u> (*Lavandula*):

The herb is known as a natural stress reliever and is used prominently in relaxation and sleep applications. In the market, there are a ton of lavender scented candles, lavender essential oil, and teas that are to be used at bedtime to help those suffering from insomnia to nod off. Furthermore, lavender can be used as a treatment for burns and as an antiseptic. For example, if you soak some flowers in water, you can then use that water to wash your face and it may help treat acne.

It can be a great addition to a garden or pots on the patio since bees love them and their flowers smell wonderful. Lavender can be grown in both gardens and in pots, but they are most impressive in a field where they can spread and cover the ground. It needs full sun and well-drained soil to grow best. Lavender is hardy, but in hot summer climates, afternoon shade may help it thrive more. Slightly alkaline soils will produce the best results.

There are pictures all over the internet showing the beauty of lavender fields. Awash with the purple color, these stand out as an oasis of beauty. But you can have a similar corner in your backyard by planting these blooming beauties that will release such a fragrance that when you visit that corner of your garden, you will simply breathe deeply and sigh.

11. <u>**Lemon Balm**</u> (*Melissa officinalis*):

Lemon balm is a member of the mint family. This lemon-scented herb can be found in oil, extract, salve, or tincture form. It is known to help ease anxiety and stress and is often used for insomnia. In addition, it has benefits for cold sores, indigestion, genital herpes, high cholesterol, and heartburn. Lemon balm has been used for centuries, even historically being steeped in wine to help lift the spirits. In addition, it can help to heal wounds and treat skin discomfort caused by insect stings or included in a cream to treat cold sores. When combined with valerian or chamomile or hops, it can be a very effective relaxation aid. The easiest application is simply to chop some lemon balm into various cooking dishes like omelets, pork, lamp, soup, fruit salads, and more.

Growing lemon balm at home is relatively easy. The plants should be initially grown indoors and transplanted outside. Plants should be placed in a shady area with partial sunshine. Barely cover the seeds and keep watering to a minimum. Once there are shoots, it can be transplanted into the garden. The soil should be kept moist.

12. <u>Marshmallow</u> (*Althaea officinalis*):

Good for alleviating allergies. The entire plant is edible, so you can toss them into a salad and brew a useful tea. As a perennial herb, marshmallow has been used as a folk remedy to treat colds and cough.

Throat lozenges that contain marshmallow root extract may help cure dry coughs and soothe an irritated throat. In fact, marshmallows that you create a s'more with exist because of this plant. The juice from the marsh mallow plant has been used for centuries as pain relief. In the 1800s, it was mixed with sugar and egg white to be a more pleasant experience for children suffering from a sore throat. It was so popular, that it was marketed as a treat. Marsh mallow is anti-inflammatory and antioxidant so it also relieves symptoms of eczema and dermatitis. An ointment containing 20% marshmallow root extract can help the affected area. This ointment may also act as antibiotic for wounds since the root may have some analgesic properties as well. Currently, there are some studies aimed at discovering the benefit of marshmallow root in repairing the lining of the intestinal tract. If you do take marshmallow root for any ailment, be sure to only take it as a supplement for one month. You then need to take a break before resuming.

Marshmallow is a perennial weed that flowers and is fond of moist, damp places. The leaves have a similar shape with a maple leaf and the flowers, usually white, mauve or pink, have five heart-shaped petals. Its flowers, leaves, and roots are edible.

13. <u>Oregano</u> (*Origanum vulgare*):

It is one of the oldest known herbs used for treating a variety of conditions. In fact, Hippocrates used it as an antiseptic. It can also be used to treat respiratory tract disorders, urinary track disorders and menstrual cramps. Topically, it can also be used to treat acne and dandruff. This popular herb is one of nature's strongest antibiotics, and some studies show it can be effective against a wide range of food pathogens. In 2014 scientists released information that some popular culinary herbs such as marjoram, oregano, and rosemary may have the potential to help manage diabetes. Lesser known uses of oregano include alleviation of muscle pain, toothaches, heart conditions, cold sores, earache, sore throat, and fatigue.

Oregano is easy to care for and can thrive either in pots or a garden setting. Make sure to put it in a warm, sunny spot with light soil. It can be a good addition to a vegetable garden as it can help to keep pests away that might impact broccoli or beans. The plants have pink flowers and can be terrific ground cover. Be careful where you plant it as it can sometimes go crazy and spread.

14. <u>Parsley</u> (*Petroselinum crispum*):

Parsley is a good source of vitamin C, vitamin K, and iron. This can improve skin health, promote faster healing of skin ailments, and strengthen immune and circulatory systems. In fact, some studies show that it has more vitamin C than an orange. Parsley is a natural antioxidant, which can help to reduce bad breath and oral infections. Parsley may help with digestion and flatulence. As it is an antibiotic and antioxidant, it may help to prevent some cancers, and treat osteoporosis and diabetes. Chopped fresh parsley applied to a new bruise may help ease pain and reduce inflammation. A great first-aid secret would be to freeze some in ice cubes to rub on bruises; the parsley helps with the bruise and the ice will reduce inflammation further. Take note that since parsley contains so much vitamin K, people who are taking blood-thinning medicine should watch consumption. Large amounts of parsley may cause uterine contractions, so pregnant women may want to avoid it also.

This biennial herb can be slow to germinate, so you can help to speed up the growth cycle by soaking the seeds in water overnight before planting. Parsley likes rich, slightly damp soil in full sun or partial shade. Parsley self-sows, so be prepared that it may spread when planting in a garden. If you do plant in a garden, good location would be close to corn, asparagus, or tomatoes. If you grow roses, you can plant near those as well. When harvesting, remember that the leaf stems have three segments. Cut leaves from the outer sections of the plant so that the inner portions can replenish and mature. You can harvest the stalks and keep them in a container of water in the refrigerator. Alternately, you can dry the leaves and use them as flavorings.

15. <u>**Peppermint**</u> (*Mentha x piperita*):

Peppermint is a hybrid of spearmint and water mint that has a wide variety of uses from mouth fresheners, dental products, soothing balms, gum, headache rubs, candies, and more. This may be one of the oldest medicinal herbs used by man. It can easily be grown in a garden where the plants are assured of sufficient water if you give it plenty of room to spread.

Sipping tea made from peppermint leaves can help calm stomach upsets and relieve pain and discomfort due to gas. Carry a few sprigs of peppermint when you travel. If you inhale the aroma of peppermint, it may help prevent nausea and vomiting associated with motion sickness. It's easy to carry a tube of peppermint essential oil when traveling via a plane or in the car if motion sickness begins.

Members of the mint family contain an ingredient called menthol, which is very aromatic and has a cooling effect on the skin. Peppermint oil is a useful ingredient in balms that treat headaches and cold symptoms. It's easy to make a poultice of peppermint leaves that can be applied on the skin which could help relieve the itch and burn from skin allergies and inflammatory conditions. Menthol has slight analgesic action, which is why it is included in balms to help relieve headaches and muscle cramps.

Mint is a perennial plant that thrives in light soil that is moist but with good drainage. Most varieties will put up with shade. If planted outside, the plants spread and will cover the ground rather easily. If planted in a garden, they should be positioned near tomatoes or cabbage. If you are growing in a pot, use compost or fertilizer every few months. Protect the plants or bring indoors during winter and cold climate. Most varieties will tolerate some shade and the variegated types may require some protection from direct sun. For growing outdoors, plant one or two purchased plants (or one or two cuttings from a friend) about 2 feet apart in moist soil. One or two plants will easily cover the ground. Mint should grow to 1 or 2 feet tall.

16. <u>Plantain</u> (*Plantago major*):

This may be popularly known as a weed, but it definitely has some medicinal uses. It can cleanse your blood, so it's good for liver health and can draw toxins out of your system. Although not native to North America, it was introduced here by settlers from Europe and Asia and can now be found in local stores. Although the leaves are edible, their flavor might not fit everyone's liking as they are more bitter than spinach.

For heartburn, indigestion, and ulcers, the leaves can also be brewed into a tea or made into a tincture. Adding plantain into an ointment can help with rashes, cuts, bruises, and insect bites. It is also known to help with indigestion, heartburn, and ulcers when taken orally. Since it is a natural antibiotic with anti-inflammatory properties, the ointment will help speed-up the recovery process. The tea or tincture can also be spread or sprayed onto insect bites to help relieve itching. For anyone who suffers from poison sumac, poison ivy, or poison oak, soaking the affected area with plantain tea will ease the suffering. Drops made from plantain can also be used to help with ear infections if the ear drum is still intact (has not burst). These drops will help to shorten the length of the infection and lessen the pain associated with it.

Greater Plantain is a low growing plant and will only reach the height of a foot or so. The plants, with little white flowers, prefers full sun or partial shade.

17. **<u>Pot Marigold</u>** (*Calendula officinalis*):

Calendula (aka "Pot Marigold") is one of the most popular edible flowers. Keep in mind that it is not in the same genus as the common marigold. However, they are part of the same family, along with daisies and chrysanthemums. The edible flowers can be used to treat a variety of problems related to the skin like sunburn, acne, blemishes, cuts, bruises, and such. It can help to stop bleeding and reduce inflammation when applied on a wound. A tea made of the steeped flowers is often ingested to get relief from digestive issues and varicose veins. In addition, calendula may help to lower a fever, ease a headache, improve circulation, and block histamines. If you add calendula into your hair rinse, it may help to cover greying hair and ease dry scalp. With great skin healing properties, calendula is a good addition to salves, body products, and soap. As its edible right out of the ground, it is easy to add to salads for simple nutrition. Many people grow pot marigolds because they are bright and cheery and bloom profusely. Most commonly, the blooms are yellow and orange, but there are more subtle colors in cream and pink. Pot marigolds will bloom throughout the growing season.

18. <u>Rosemary</u> (*Rosmarinus officinalis*):

Rosemary is more of a shrub than an herb, but still is an impressive plant for the aroma, the flavor, and the health benefits. Anyone who has ever bought a rosemary tree around Christmas time can attest to the terrific aroma that surrounds the plant. Belonging to the mint family, rosemary is primarily used for general wellbeing, but not for specific diseases.

Some studies indicate rosemary helps to prevent the formation of carcinogens caused by grilling foods. Thus, it's a great addition to grilled chicken, pork, or lamb. It is also known to cleanse and detox the body and fight cirrhosis. Rosemary can be used as an antiseptic and as an ingredient in antibacterial agents.

Recent research in rosemary, specifically the carnosic acid of the plant, indicates that it may improve the brain and address some memory issues. Rosemary oil plays a role in similar studies.

Rosemary can be grown in a pot or planted as an aromatic hedge along a garden. In a garden, they do well around sage, carrots, cabbage, and beans. In a pot, remember that rosemary is a shrub, so it will grow taller than a typical houseplant; make sure that the plant does not become pot-bound. Leaves can easily be harvested and used in cooking and herbal teas. this grows best in hot and dry climates.

19. <u>Sage</u> (*Salvia officinalis*):

Research indicates that sage might improve memory and reduce inflammation. In addition, sage can serve as a natural aid in combating anxiety and nervous disorders, improve appetite, and prevent flatulence. Luckily, it tastes great in a lot of dishes and can easily be incorporated into cooking dishes.

Sage may have a hormone regulatory effect on women. A tea made from the leaves can be used to relieve symptoms of menstrual pain, PMS, and menopause. Asthma might be treated by inhaling an infusion of sage. Alzheimer's, dementia, and depression might be alleviated by sage as well.

Sage is a great herb to use in cooking and is easy to grow, even in small containers in your kitchen. Over-watering is the biggest threat because sage doesn't like wet ground and mildew is a concern. Sage will produce the most flavorful leaves when it receives a lot of sunlight. If planted in an herb garden, it performs well when planted near strawberries, carrots, cabbage, and tomatoes. With slightly alkaline soil and infrequent fertilization, sage will grow a little slower but will provide a more intense flavor. Containers should be placed in an area with medium to full sun exposure.

20. <u>St. John's Wort</u> (*Hypericum perforatum*):

Although popular as an antidepressant, this herb can also help with back pain. It can help to alleviate feelings of sadness, grief, depression, and Seasonal Affective Disorder. But it should be used carefully as it can interact with certain prescription drugs. Luckily, unlike a lot of herbal remedies, there is a lot of scientific studies and information on this particular herb. Your medical doctor might even recommend taking this for minor bouts of depression.

It is typically found in oil, capsule, tincture, or raw form. St. John's wort contains bioflavonoids and antioxidants that can affect chemical and hormonal balances in the body. For the anti-depressant aspects, this herb contains a chemical that may delay or completely inhibit neurotransmitters in the brain such as dopamine, serotonin, and norepinephrine. In this same regard, St. John's wort can also help with anxiety by changing the hormonal balance in the body. This can help with irritability, sleep disturbances, metabolism, and chronic fatigue. By helping to eliminate cortisol and other stress hormones, overall health can improve. As it changes the hormonal balance, it is thought to help women with PMS and menopause symptoms as well, lessening the anxiety and mood swings that can occur.

Further studies are being conducted on the benefits of St. John's wort for those suffering from addiction and withdrawal. Some data has shown that this herb may be helpful for those quitting addictive substances such as alcohol or nicotine. In addition, further studies are being done into the antiviral abilities of this herb as well.

For gardening, St. John's Wort isn't particularly about the soil type and adapts to both dry or moist soil, even if it has to tolerate a drought or soggy conditions occasionally. Plant the herb in a location with a nice balance of shade and sun – too much shade and you won't get enough flowers. When planting, make sure you know that there is a potential for photo-toxicity so grazing animals should be kept away.

21. <u>Thyme</u> (*Thymus linearis*):

This lovely smelling herb attracts bees and is a pretty addition to any garden. It spreads easily and is hardy.

It has pretty purple flowers. Can be used to treat colds and the flu. With disinfectant properties, it is useful as a gargle for a sore throat. In fact, thyme essential oil is often used as a natural cough remedy. As an alternative, drinking thyme tea may help a sore throat as well.

Thyme is full of vitamin C and is a good source of vitamin A. So, adding thyme to your diet may help boost your immune system and fight off colds.

Essential oil of thyme may be a natural way to fight off mold in your house and can be used as a disinfectant. You can also make a homemade insect repellant out of thyme oil by making a mixture of olive oil and thyme oil in a 1:4 ratio. You can substitute water for the olive oil, but it will not be as structured. In fact, a mixture of thyme oil and olive oil as a moisturizer may boost your mood and increase your positive feelings.

As thyme is frequently used in cooking, you will find this herb in a lot of herb gardens. It can tolerate indirect light, which means it can even be grown inside those little kitchen herb gardens. The pot should have sufficient drainage as thyme doesn't like wet roots. Allow the pot to dry out in between watering. Keep the woody stems cut back to encourage new growth and when the flowers come, trim them and dry for use as a tea. Removing the flowers will only increase production. During the summer, you can set the plants outside to get some extra sunshine and fresh air, but make sure you give it time to acclimate to the different lighting conditions. Trim the stems and remove the leaves by running your fingers down the stem in the opposite direction of growth. Chop leaves and use as seasoning.

22. <u>Valerian</u> (*Valeriana officinalis*):

Lovely and useful. Typically associated with supplements to help you relax and sleep, either in capsule or tea form. It can be used to reduce feelings of anxiety and reduce pain. Precautions on most bottles of Valerian indicate that you should not be taking a daily dose for more than one month at a time. In addition, a variety of other uses have been showing up. Studies indicate that a psychoactive compound present in valerian root may help to reduce or relieve anxiety. This herb may also be useful in reducing the symptoms of ADHD (attention deficit hyperactivity disorder) as it contains the ability to energize a chemical in the brain known as GABA; it may affect OCD symptoms as well. Menopause symptoms may be lessened with the use of valerian as it may help to reduce hot flashes. Valerian may improve your blood flow, strengthening your blood vessel pliability, and improving the heart muscle; and as it is a sedative, it will improve your heart rate. Users of the supplement have indicated that it has helped with Restless Leg Syndrome and studies are being conducted to find out if this is a consistent health benefit.

It is a perennial plant that has white flowers that attract bees and butterflies to your garden. The plant must have full sun exposure for about six (6) hours a day. It likes a well-draining, nitrogen-rich soil but appreciates plenty of moisture. Give the plants plenty of space as they can grow to about five (5) feet high and as much as 12 inches wide. Harvest time is usually the best in spring and fall.

23. <u>Yarrow</u> (*Achillea millefolium*):

Useful in treating wounds, reducing fevers, alleviate allergies, and fight colds. This herb can induce sweating.

This is another ancient herbal treatment possibly dating back to 1000 BC and closely related to another common herbal medicine, chamomile. It boosts the immune system and can soothe cold symptoms. It is considered as an astringent, antiseptic, and anti-inflammatory agent. Tea helps digestion and upset stomach. Topically, the essential oil can reduce eczema related pain, itching, and swelling. Yarrow in boiling water creates a steam that can be inhaled to help clear congestion and control coughing. It is sometimes used as a sedative to help relieve symptoms of insomnia or anxiety. Historically, this herb was consumed like a vegetable and was eaten and prepared like spinach. As a seasoning, it can be used as an alternative to tarragon because the flavor is similar. In powdered form, yarrow can be spread onto a wound to help stop bleeding and lessen pain. Since it's a natural antiseptic, it will keep the wound from getting infected. A poultice made from yarrow has been known to help breast-feeding women who are suffering from mastitis, providing quick relieve for the pain of cracked nipples. Yarrow may have some digestive benefits by lessening cramps, flatulence, or diarrhea by reducing muscle spasms along the GI tract. It also has cardiovascular benefits because it helps to lower blood pressure and improve the respiratory system, alleviating asthma symptoms.

Yarrow is versatile and hardy perennial. It has showy flower heads that are made up of a bunch of tiny, tightly-packed flowers. These flowers may be pink, red, yellow, or a number of shades in between. It is a nice addition to the garden, as it attracts butterflies, smells nice, and is drought-resistant.

The herb should be planted in the spring because it likes hot and dry conditions. Make sure that the soil is well-drained. Soil should be average because if it is too rich, your growth will take over and you'll be required to trim it regularly. Put the plants about 12-24 inches apart as they will spread and grow to about four (4) feet tall. In the spring, a thin layer of compost will help them grow.

Chapter 3: Beneficial Herbs to Add to Your Medicine Chest

Herb	Description of Benefits
abscess root	May reduce fever, treat cough or reduce inflammation.
agrimony	Improves vision, can help to heal wounds, ease digestive issues, treat cough and sore throat, or as a sleep aid. Primarily used as a tea.
alder buckthorn	Used as a laxative; dangerous in large doses.
aniseed	Digestive aid (reduces gas and eases nausea) and increases milk supply in breastfeeding women. Can help to alleviate anxiety and ease cold symptoms.
arnica	Anti-inflammatory. It should not be taken internally but is beneficial as an ointment for reducing the appearance of bruises and mild muscle pain.

Herb	Description of Benefits
asafetida	May be useful in treating breathing problems, IBS or high cholesterol.
ashwagandha	Best-known to boost sexual drive and fertility. Also known to enhance memory, boost energy, and help to alleviate stress and anxiety.
aspalathus	Antioxidant similar to bilberry. Boosts eye health and immune function.
astragalus	Strengthens the immune system.
Avaram Senna	Has laxative properties, eases conjunctivitis, treats diabetes, and alleviates urinary tract issues.
balloon flower	Anti-microbial, anti-inflammatory, relieves allergies, improves insulin levels, lowers cholesterol.
belladonna	Although toxic, this has been used by women to enlarge their pupils to enhance beauty (the translation is "beautiful woman"). Can be included in small dosages as a sedative.

Herb	Description of Benefits
bilberry	A powerful antioxidant that is relatively unknown. It has positive effects on the brain and heart. Protects the retina and improves vision.
bilwa	Used in India to help treat eye conditions (sties and conjunctivitis).
bitter orange	Alleviates nausea, constipation, and indigestion.
bitter melon	Helps reduce blood glucose levels.
black cohosh	Anti-inflammatory and rejuvenating herb with immune-boosting properties. Popular in supplements for women to combat menstrual and menopausal complications. Also believed to improve good circulation, help lower blood pressure, and improve heart health. Should not be used by pregnant or nursing women.

Herb	Description of Benefits
black walnut	This herb has been used as an anti-parasitic, anti-fungal, digestive aid, and cure poison ivy, and treatment for warts.
blue snakeweed	May ease malaria symptoms; treats dysentery, livery disorders, may control diabetes; anti-inflammatory properties.
borage	Used to alleviate colic, cramps, diarrhea, urinary tract disorders.
burdock	Used as a diuretic; lowers blood sugar and eases symptoms of the common cold.
cardamom	Anti-microbial properties. Can rid the blood of bad cholesterol and improve circulation. May serve as an anti-depressant, anti-inflammatory, and anti-spasmodic. Can improve the health and function of male sexual organs.

Herb	Description of Benefits
catnip	Can be a digestive aid (reduces gas). The tea can relieve cold symptoms and reduce fever by inducing sweating. When applied to wounds, it can help stop bleeding and reduce swelling. Easy to grow and produces beautiful purple flowers.
charcoal tree	May be used to treat a sore throat, toothaches, bronchitis, asthma, and gonorrhea. And may be beneficial as a general antidote to general poisoning.
chasteberry	Used for hundreds of years to control female hormone imbalances (combatting PMS, breast tenderness, hot flashes, mood swings, and boosting milk production in lactating mothers).
chickweed	Relieves itchy skin, remedy for pulmonary diseases, may help with anemia, bronchitis, RA and menstrual pain.

Herb	Description of Benefits
cinnamon	Can be used to treat minor wounds as an anti-bacterial agent and can be an ingredient in anti-viral topical treatments and oral remedies.
cinquefoil	Reduces inflammation, helps to alleviate jaundice, treats ulcers and mouth sores.
clove bud	Enhances the immune system as it is an antioxidant, anti-bacterial and anti-microbial agent. May treat toothaches.
comfrey	Reduces inflammation and relieves digestive issues.
common nettle	Treat kidney and UT disorders, symptoms of gout, and the flu.

Herb	Description of Benefits
coriander	The seeds help to balance blood sugar by stimulating the pancreas to produce insulin. Coriander can also help liver function and improves cholesterol levels. It is a natural antibiotic, so it could help in the treatment of food-borne pathogens (such as salmonella). Good source of fiber, vitamins A and K, antioxidants, potassium, iron, and magnesium.
cranberry	Anyone who has ever had a bladder infection can use cranberry supplements but can also be used to fight prostatitis.
cypress	Antiseptic and astringent. The prime ingredient in natural sedatives and respiratory mixtures. Also used as a diuretic.
daisy	Treats disorders of the respiratory or GI tract.
dill	Ease upset stomach, help to alleviate insomnia, may treat colic.

Herb	Description of Benefits
elderberry	Historically, the flowers have been used in flu remedies and antiviral mixes (topical and oral). Can treat pain, reduce swelling, alleviate coughs, fevers, constipation, and sinus infections.
eucalyptus	Antiviral, antibacterial, and anti-infectious properties. This herb is a well-known component of a lot of cold remedies.
evening primrose	The oil used as an anti-inflammatory and can help with eczema.
fenugreek	May help with diabetes, menopause, and digestive ailments.
garden angelic	Alleviate disorders of the GI tract, fevers, infections, and symptoms of the flu.
geranium	Can detoxify the liver and stop the bleeding of wounds. It is also an antibacterial and anti-infectious agent.

Herb	Description of Benefits
ginkgo biloba	Improves blood flow to the eyes (helps with macular degeneration). May help ears by preventing tinnitus, inner ear disturbances, and other conditions. Can help with asthma, bronchitis, fatigue, or Alzheimer's.
ginseng	Relieves and prevents fatigue (mental and physical). Reduces the severity and frequency of colds. Possibly beneficial to those suffering from erectile dysfunction.
goldenrod	Treats painful menstrual cramps; externally can be applied to eczema and skin ulcers.
goldenseal	Reduces the inflammation associated with conjunctivitis and sties.
greenthread	(aka Navajo tea) A diuretic, anti-inflammatory, natural remedy for urinary tract infections, and sooths gastrointestinal distress.

Herb	Description of Benefits
hepatica (common)	Treats liver disease; eases bronchitis and gout.
hibiscus	Boosts fluid balance in the body, maintains normal body temperature, and enhances heart health.
hollyhock (common)	Used as a laxative and controls inflammation
hops	Associated with beer-making, hops can also be used to induce sleep, alleviate stress, and lessen menopause issues (hot flashes and others).
horse chestnut	Extract from the seed can be used to treat varicose veins, reduce swelling in the feet and legs.
horsetail	Heals ulcers, treat wounds, kidney problems, and can help to stop bleeding.

Herb	Description of Benefits
hyssop	An anti-microbial agent that treats respiratory infections and skin conditions. Fights fungal infections, the flu, and strep. This herb has been around a long time and is one of the oldest known medicinal herbs. Closely related to marjoram and oregano.
Indian sandalwood	Treats urinary tract infections, common cold, bronchitis, fever, and gallbladder disorders.
karvy	Anti-microbial, anti-inflammatory (may help with RA)
kava	Relieves anxiety with significant muscle-relaxing effects. May also be used to treat urinary tract infections or asthma.
kratom	Has gained popularity recently as an aid to relieve withdrawal symptoms for people suffering from addiction.
licorice	Treat sore throats and cough, calms gastrointestinal tract issues.

Herb	Description of Benefits
lovage	Serves as a digestive aid (reduces gas), eases a sore throat, eases pain from stomach ulcers. Can be added to a bath to ease pain and inflammation resulting from skin conditions. Belongs to the carrot family.
Mahonia grape extract	Reduces the impact of sun damage on the eyes while helping to strengthen the retina, can slow eye aging and improve overall eye health.
marjoram	Possesses antibacterial and anti-infectious properties. May soothe sore muscles and regulate blood pressure.
milk thistle	Remedy for kidney problems. Can be used to alleviate the harmful effects of exposure to environmental toxins and alcohol poisoning.

Herb	Description of Benefits
myrrh	One of the oldest known herbs and was mentioned in the Christian Bible. Can soothe skin rashes, impair nerve spasms, and boost the immune system. An anti-infectious and antiviral agent.
neem	Used to treat worms, skin infections, malaria, and RA.
noni	May relieve joint pain and skin conditions.
passionflower	Assists with vision issues. Helps to alleviate eye strain if you spend all day staring at a screen. Relaxes the small blood vessels in the eye. Thought to have some anti-depressant properties.
pennyroyal	Eases headaches and colic lessens feverish symptoms
poppy	Soothes coughs, promotes sleep, eases asthma and whooping cough
primrose	Promotes sleep, reduces tension, eases headaches, and treats gout.

Herb	Description of Benefits
purslane	Anti-bacterial and anti-fungal properties.
red clover	Detoxifies the blood and body. The tea can be an effective treatment for cold symptoms.
rosewood	Fights infections, both bacterial and viral.
slippery elm	Approved by the FDA to treat minor throat irritations and a cough resulting from a cold or heartburn.
spearmint	Aids in treating bronchial problems and nervous system issues.
summer savory	Anti-bacterial and anti-fungal uses.
sweet cicely	Known as Spanish Chervil and Garden Myrrh. Can be used as a natural sweetener. It may also treat anxiety and hypertension, ease digestive problems, and detoxify the urinary tract.

Herb	Description of Benefits
sweet marjoram	High in beneficial nutrients such as vitamins A, C, K, iron, potassium, calcium, zinc, magnesium, and manganese. Anti-microbial and aids with digestion.
sweet violet	Alleviates cold and flu symptoms. Serves as a pain reliever for headaches and muscle soreness. Can help detoxify (diuretic). Relaxant and sleep aid.
tarragon	Treats toothaches, may induce menstruation, and eliminate parasites in the intestines.
tea tree	Has an antibiotic property that treats oral and skin issues. Possibly in the top 10 most frequently used herbs as it is added to cosmetic applications as well (shampoo, conditioner, lotions, etc.)
turmeric	Digestive aid, improves liver function and relieves pain associated with arthritis.

Herb	Description of Benefits
verbena	Treat respiratory tract diseases and sore throats.
veronica	Treats sinus and ear infections.
watercress	Diuretic and anti-bacterial.
water germander	Eases symptoms from asthma, fever, hemorrhoids, intestinal parasites, and diarrhea.
white buttercup	Ailments for GI and respiratory diseases and may inhibit fungal activity.
white willow	The precursor of aspirin as a source of salicylic acid.
yellow lady's slipper	Remedy for anxiety, headaches, toothache, and can be used as a sedative.

Chapter 4: How to Prepare Herbs

The time and method of harvesting greatly depends on the type of herb you are harvesting. Some medicinal supplements are sourced from the flowers, some on the seeds, and some on the roots – and some on any and all parts of the plant. Generally, the leaves should be harvested before flowers form. After flowering, a lot of herbs become bitter or their flavors are greatly diminished. When the leaves are harvested, it is actually the oil in the leaves which provides both the fragrance and flavor. Ideally, the leaves should be picked early in the morning before temperatures rise. The leaves should not be washed as that will rinse away the useful oils in the herbs.

For the flowers, some herbs like chamomile and lavender are best when harvested before the flowers fully blooms. When harvesting for seeds, herbs such as coriander, fennel, and caraway need to be harvested just as the pods begin changing colors. For herbs where the roots are most useful, most of those need to be harvested at the end of summer or early autumn. Harvesting annuals can be ongoing and can be done right until frost occurs. However, for perennials, trimming should not occur any later than the dog days of summer as this may encourage new growth that will continue after the season and cold weather that can damage the plant. It pays to know your plants as certain flowering herbs such as tarragon or lavender should be cut back to half their height in early July in order to promote a second bloom in autumn.

Herbs Preservation

Typically, herbs are best used when fresh, especially when cooking. After an herb is picked, the aroma and flavor fade quickly. Once harvested, there are a number of ways to store and preserve herbs for future use. A lot of herbs like parsley, basil, cilantro, and basil can be stored on the kitchen counter in a glass of water. Just like an arrangement of fresh flowers. Trim the ends of the stems and give them an inch or two of water to feed them. Those types of herbs will remain fresh for about a week in this fashion. For others, such as chives, thyme, and rosemary, they are best stored in a refrigerator. Herbs should be wrapped in a damp towel and stored in the refrigerator. There are also a number of storage containers available on the market that can help to prolong the life of fresh herbs. None of the herbs should be rinsed off before they are stored because this will diminish their flavor and hasten wilting. In addition, the longer herbs are stored, the less their potency will be.

Drying your herbs will allow you the longest storage length and will retain the highest quality and flavor. Stored properly, dried herbs can be flavorful and helpful for 24-36 months but are most potent within 12 months. For long term storage, and to retain the highest flavor and quality, consider drying herbs. Dried herbs can be kept for two or three years but should really be used within a year. Any storage time longer than this, will cause the decline of taste and aroma. Sun, oven, or dehydrator drying is not recommended, because the herbs will lose too much flavor and color.

When using an oven, the temperature should be set between 180 and 200 degrees only. Keep the door open in order to let moisture escape. You must watch the herbs closely and repeatedly stir the layer of herbs to ensure they dry completely and do not burn. For a dehydrator, a machine will quickly work on drying the herbs – although the racks may need to be rotated to ensure all of the batches are dried evenly. The sun can dry herbs as well but it will need a little longer drying time and a structure may have to be build that will help to ensure that the herbs don't blow away and remain bug-free. Air-drying is another method. Gather the herbs by the stems and hang them upside-down in a warm area (at least 70 degrees F). Make sure the area is not in direct sunlight, but the herbs will take about three (3) weeks to be ready. Be aware that you can minimize the mess this method makes by placing a paper bag over any herbs with seed heads as the seeds will drop into the bag as they dry instead of on the floor. This method will take further processing once the herbs are dried, the leaves will need to be removed and crushed or ground into powder just before use. Some people who use this method frequently will take a picture frame and cover it with netting or screen and use those to hold the herbs while drying. Leaves should be striped and laid in a single-layer on the screen, turning the frame every day. Microwave ovens can also be used for drying. Once the herbs are cleaned, they should be laid in a single-layer on a paper towel and heated in 30 second bursts until they are dry. Great care should be taken and the herbs should not be set on fire. Regardless of which method you use, once herbs are dried and prepared, they should be stored in an airtight container, preferably ceramic or glass. Keep the container away from heat or light. A lot of people keep spices near the stove for the convenience of cooking, but that quickly lessens flavor and fragrance. If possible, keep the leaves whole and crush it just before consumption.

Freezing herbs are another method to preserve herbs for future use. Unlike drying, these herbs should be washed before processing. Once dry, they should be spread into a single layer and placed in the freezer. Once frozen, they can be combined into a container and placed back into the freezer until ready for use. Some herbs freeze better than others and some research should be done to ensure it is the correct approach. Sage, tarragon, dill, basil, chives, thyme, mint, and others will freeze well and remain viable for up to six months. As an alternative approach, you can try painting the leaves with oil, then freeze them. Afterwards, take them out and chop them in a food processor with a little oil to form a paste. The paste can then be frozen either in a block or in small segments (such as a tablespoon or ice-cube tray) so that when cooking, you can easily remove some of the paste and add to soups or stews. If you don't want to add the oil, you can simply add chopped herbs to water and freeze in smaller sections.

Herbal salts can be created by combining salt and spices. Using a glass jar with a lid, simply layer the leaves of the herb with layers of salt, pressing firmly between layers until the jar is full. Seal tightly. Or combine 1 cup of salt with six (6) tablespoons of an herb in a food processor and process until combined. This herbal salt can be stored in an air-tight container. The flavor will be most viable for the first year and will diminish after that.

<u>Harvesting and Growth</u>

As a general rule, when harvesting, you should never take more than a third of the entire growth. This will allow enough of the plant material to remain so that effective regrowth can occur. Although this rule may apply in most cases, some plants are exceptions. For example, chives will grow back faster if they are cut down to less than an inch of exposure from the ground. Other species flourish if they are harvested all at once. Some harvests are based on the time of year, some are based on the size of the plant, some are based on the coloring of the leaves, and others are based on when blooms appear.

Each plant has its own preferred method of harvesting. Annuals that are leafy, like basil, should be harvested by pinching bunches of leaves off the stems from the tips. They should be clipped close to encourage regrowth and more prolific plants. Any herbs that have a longer stem like rosemary, parsley, and lavender, should be cut down next to the base, less than an inch from the ground cover. Perennial herbs that are leafy, like tarragon, sage, oregano, and thyme, can be picked by the stem.

Some plants are harvested to use more than one part – the leaves, the seeds or the roots. For some of those herbs, timing can be everything. Cilantro's leaves are the part of the plant that is being used so it should be harvested before blooming. If you are after coriander, it involves waiting for that same plant to bloom and produce seeds. Those seeds are then harvested to become coriander. Herbs that are based on the flower should be harvested just before the blooms fully open so that they are most potent.

To produce more leaves on herbs like dill or basil requires removal of the flower stalks once they appear. Herbs that bloom, like mint, thyme or oregano, are at their most flavorful just before they begin to bloom, so that is the best time to harvest their leaves.

Herbs can either be grown from seeds or harvested to be grown from the clippings; stalks should be placed in water until they grow roots and then can be transplanted into pots or directly into the garden.

Multiple Uses

Oil and Butter: Combining herbs with butter or olive oil can not only serve to preserve the herbs, it can also be a great addition to cooking. This mixture will cut down on the herbs discoloring or wilting. To ensure the safest preparation method, the herbs must not have any water at the time the mixture is made. If the herbs have any water, it will increase the risk of bacterial contamination.

Vinegars: Herbs can also be preserved by creating flavored vinegar. Mild vinegars work best, like white, rice or white wine. However, for stronger flavored herbs like basil or rosemary, apple cider vinegar can be used for a new flavor combination. Put fresh herbs into containers of vinegar, add a lid, and simply wait until infusion.

Chapter 5: Conclusion

When deciding which herbs to grow, there are multiple factors that should come into play. First is the climate in the area you live in and your gardening abilities. There is nothing more frustrating than trying to grow something that just won't sprout. Then, how much time do you want to devote to the growing, harvesting, and preparation of the herbs? Do you want to get involved in drying and mixing tinctures? Finally, what medicinal conditions do you want to treat – if you suffer from back pain, then maybe you want to focus on those herbs that are helpful in treating inflammation.

As with anything else, it pays to do your research and be informed. The medical condition may be something serious enough to warrant any attempt to cure it. Herbal supplements cover a wide variety of treatments for conditions such a migraine, cold, high blood pressure, and more. Unfortunately, there isn't a lot of reliable scientific studies that have reliably been conducted on how effective herbs can be used as medicine and what the side effects might be. While most manufacturers of herbal supplements meet consistent quality standards, it pays to be informed as to what brands are of high quality because those companies do not need to get approval from the Food and Drug Administration (FDA) before marketing their products. In fact, even when the FDA gets involved, herbal supplements fall under the category of dietary supplements which gives them a different set of rules from food or drug approval. Companies are not allowed to make a scientific or medical claim and must put a disclaimer about any evaluation of any claims for treating conditions.

Notwithstanding regulations and quality concerns, herbal supplements can have powerful effects on the body. Some can interact with prescription medications currently being uses. And some can be more harmful than beneficial when taken in the wrong dosages. Medications such as blood pressure medications or blood thinners may interact with a variety of herbal supplements. If you are currently breast-feeding or pregnant, you should definitely do your research and speak with your physician about any supplements and side effects. If you're having surgery, it is essential that you tell your doctor what herbal medicine you're taking to ensure that your surgeons have all the information necessary to ensure your safety.

When starting a new supplement, do your research and find out the side effects. Begin by taking the lowest recommended dosage and keep track of what your taking and any affects you may be feeling. Choose a brand that has been tested by reputable independent sources and laboratories. Check for any advisors which would indicate adverse effects of the supplement; the FDA website typically contains updates.

Thanks for making it through to the end of *Herbal Apothecary*, let's hope it was informative and was able to provide you with all of the tools you need to achieve your goals whatever they may be.

Finally, if you found this book useful in any way, a review on Amazon is always appreciated!

This book belongs to a series of books about herbal medicine and how to use it to improve our life. For more information, visit **www.db-publishing.com**